EVERY DAY *is*
MOTHER'S
DAY!

Published in 2011 by Prion
an imprint of the Carlton Publishing Group
20 Mortimer Street
London W1T 3JW

ISBN 978-1-85375-833-1

A CIP catalogue record of this book can be obtained from the British Library.

10 9 8 7 6 5 4 3 2 1

Printed in China

EVERY DAY *is*
MOTHER'S
DAY!

500 Witty Quotes
Celebrating Mums and Motherhood

Molly Miller

Happy Mothers' Day!

Mother. Everybody has one and none of us would be here without her. After bringing us into the world she takes on so many roles – nursemaid, peacemaker, cleaner, cook, teacher, advisor, confidant and, above all, best friend forever.

This book celebrates the most important (and underappreciated!) job in the world with the wise and witty words of mothers and their children across the years – from Jane Austen to Britney Spears.

There's warmth and humour on every page as a host of celebrities pour out their hearts and minds on such subjects as baby's first words, being a working mum, hyper-active children and the limitless nature of a mother's love.

> **It is not until you become a mother that your judgement slowly turns to compassion and understanding.**
>
> Erma Bombeck

There is a widespread feeling that we have to do it all alone, and if we don't know something, or can't manage it, or, heaven forbid, don't want to, there is something lacking in our makeup.

Sally Placksin

Sometimes the laughter in mothering is the recognition of the ironies and absurdities. Sometimes, though, it's just pure, unthinking delight.

Barbara Schapiro

The art of making a mistake is crucial to motherhood. To be effective and gain the respect she needs to function, a mother must have her children believe she has never engaged in sex, never made a bad decision, never caused her own mother a moment's anxiety, and was never a child.

Erma Bombeck

It will be gone before you know it. The fingerprints on the wall appear higher and higher. Then suddenly they disappear.

Dorothy Evslin

When I pick up one of my children and cuddle them, all the strain and stress of life temporarily disappears. There is nothing more wonderful than motherhood and no one will ever love you as much as a small child.

Nicola Horlick

Sometimes the strength of motherhood is greater than natural laws.

Barbara Kingsolver

'It's hard enough to adjust [to the lack of control] in the beginning,' says a corporate vice president and single mother. 'But then you realize that everything keeps changing, so you never regain control.'

Anne C. Weisberg and Carol A. Buckler

For a parent, it's hard to recognize the significance of your work when you're immersed in the mundane details. Few of us, as we run the bathwater or spread the peanut butter on the bread, proclaim proudly, 'I'm making my contribution to the future of the planet.'

Joyce Maynard

If evolution really works how come mothers only have two hands?

Ed Dussault

A woman has two smiles that an angel might envy, the smile that accepts a lover before words are uttered, and the smile that lights on the first-born babe, and assures it of a mother's love.

Thomas C. Haliburton

Women's courage is rather different from men's. The fact that women have to bring up children and look after husbands makes them braver at facing long-term issues, such as illness.

Mary Wesley

The heart of a mother is a deep abyss at the bottom of which you will always find forgiveness.

Honoré de Balzac

I will fight for my children on any level so they can reach their potential as human beings and in their public duties.

Princess Diana

A mother is the truest friend we have, when trials heavy and sudden, fall upon us... [she will] endeavour by her kind precepts and counsels to dissipate the clouds of darkness, and cause peace to return to our hearts.

Washington Irving

There's a lot more to being a woman than being a mother, but there's a lot more to being a mother than most people suspect.

Roseanne Barr

A mother is not a person to lean on but a person to make leaning unnecessary.

Dorothy Fisher

A mother's arms are made of tenderness and children sleep soundly in them.

Victor Hugo

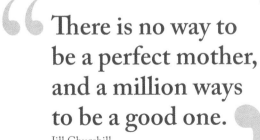

" There is no way to be a perfect mother, and a million ways to be a good one. "

Jill Churchill

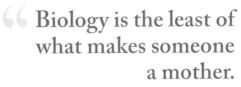

Biology is the least of
what makes someone
a mother.

Oprah Winfrey

You never realize how much your mother loves you till
you explore the attic – and find every letter you ever sent
her, every finger painting, clay pot, bead necklace, Easter
chicken, cardboard Santa Claus, paperlace Mother's Day
card and school report since day one.

Pam Brown

Mothers' love is peace. It need not be acquired, it
need not be deserved.

Erich Fromm

Most mothers are instinctive philosophers.

Harriet Beecher Stowe

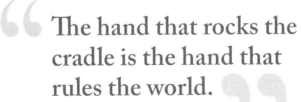

The hand that rocks the
cradle is the hand that
rules the world.

William Ross Wallace

Mother: The most beautiful word on the lips of mankind.

Kahlil Gibran

What the mother sings to the cradle goes all the way down to the coffin.
Henry Ward Beecher

(Everybody knows that a good mother gives her children a feeling of trust and stability... Somehow even her clothes feel different to her children's hands from anybody else's clothes. Only to touch her skirt or her sleeve makes a troubled child feel better.

Katharine Butler Hathaway

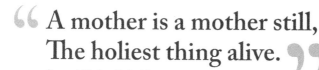

A mother is a mother still, The holiest thing alive.

Samuel Taylor Coleridge

We really have no definition of mother in our law books. Mother was believed to have been so basic that no definition was deemed necessary.

Marianne O. Battani

I would rather be the child of a mother who has all the inner conflicts of the human being than be mothered by someone for whom all is easy and smooth, who knows all the answers, and is a stranger to doubt.

D.W.Winnicott

A mother is a woman with a twenty-five-hour day who can still find time to play with her family.

Mildred B.Vermont

A mother is she who can take the place of all others, but whose place no one else can take.

Iris Peck

She discovered with great delight that one does not love one's children just because they are one's children but because of the friendship formed while raising them.

Gabrel García Márquez

I am my kid's mom.

Dr Laura Schlessinger

That dear octopus from whose tentacles we never quite escape, nor in our innermost hearts never quite wish to.

Dodie Smith

Fortunately for those who pay their court through such foibles, a fond mother, though, in pursuit of praise for her children, the most rapacious of human beings, is likewise the most credulous; her demands are exorbitant; but she will swallow anything.

Jane Austen

" A mother's love, in a degree, sanctifies the most worthless offspring. "

Hosea Ballou

A good marriage is at least 80 per cent good luck in finding the right person at the right time. The rest is trust.

Nanette Newman

Motherhood is never being number one in your list of priorities and not minding at all.

Jasmine Guinness

Nothing will ever make you as happy or sad, as
proud or as tired as motherhood.

Elia Parsons

Whenever I date a guy, I think, is this
the man I want my kids to spend their
weekends with?

Rita Rudner

Of all the rights of woman, the
greatest is to be a mother.

Lyn Yutang

There comes a time when a woman needs to stop focusing on her looks and
focus her energies on raising her children. This time comes at the moment of
conception. A child needs a role model, not a super model.

Astrid Alauda

Making the decision to have a child is momentous. It is
to decide for ever to have your heart go walking around
outside your body.

Elizabeth Stone

I want to have children and I know my time is running
out. I want to have them while my parents are still young
enough to take care of them.

Rita Rudner

> **Think of stretch marks as pregnancy service stripes.**
> Joyce Armor

I am so ready to be a mommy. I can't wait! I notice every little baby dress, every little baby toy, every little baby thing.
Halle Berry

You do a lot of growing up when you're pregnant. It's suddenly like, 'Yikes. Here it is, folks. Playtime is over.'
Connie Fioretto

> **If pregnancy were a book they would cut the last two chapters.**
> Nora Ephron

If I had my life to live over, instead of wishing away nine months of pregnancy, I'd have cherished every moment and realized that the wonderment growing inside me was the only chance in life to assist God in a miracle.
Erma Bombeck

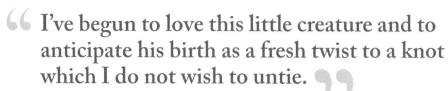

" I've begun to love this little creature and to anticipate his birth as a fresh twist to a knot which I do not wish to untie. "

Mary Wollestonecraft Shelley

Pregnancy is not a disease. It is the ultimate manifestation of health.

Laura Shanley

Suddenly she was here. And I was no longer pregnant; I was a mother. I never believed in miracles before.

Ellen Greene

Advice to expectant mothers: you must remember that when you are pregnant, you are eating for two. But you must also remember that the other one of you is about the size of a golf ball, so let's not go overboard with it. I mean a lot of pregnant women eat as though the other person they're eating for is Orson Welles.

Dave Barry

My mother groaned, my father wept, into the dangerous world I leapt; helpless, naked, piping loud, like a fiend hid in cloud.

William Blake

There is power that comes to women when they give birth. They don't ask for it, it simply invades them. Accumulates like clouds on the horizon and passes through, carrying the child with it.

Sheryl Feldman

There is no finer investment for any community than putting milk into babies.

Winston Churchill

May earth provide us with all the things of our requirements just like a mother who breastfeeds her child.

Atharva Veda

There's an African story of birth where the women gather and send you across the river, and as you walk across this log across the river you head out with these women. As you go across on the narrowest part you're alone. No one can be there with you, and as you emerge on to the other side of the river, all the women who have ever given birth are there to greet you.

Liz Koch

My opinion is that anyone offended by breastfeeding is staring too hard.

Dave Allen

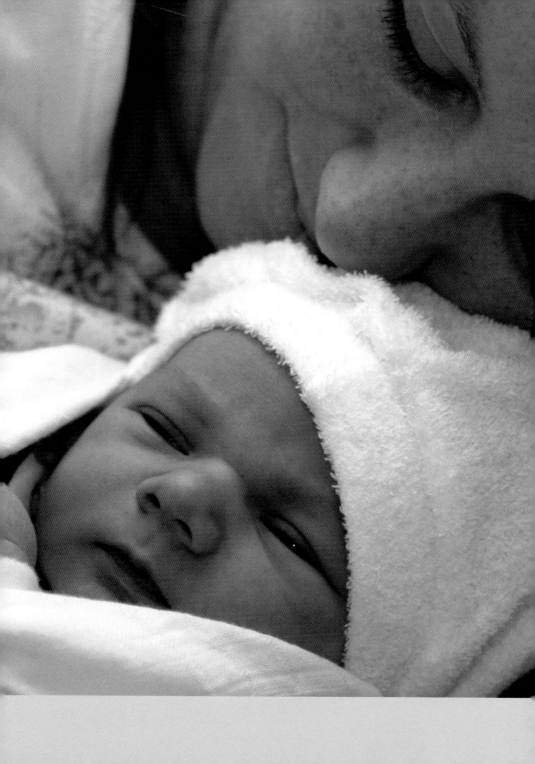

A babe at the breast is as much pleasure as the bearing is pain.
Marion Zimmer Bradley

I remember leaving the hospital thinking, 'Wait, are they just going to let me walk off with him? I don't know beans about babies. I don't have a licence to do this.'
Anne Tyler

Whenever I held my newborn baby in my arms, I used to think that what I said and did to him could have an influence not only on him but on all whom he met, not only for a day or a month or a year, but for all eternity – a very challenging and exciting thought for a mother.
Rose Kennedy

I visited those friends who'd just had a baby, and she was washing dishes and he was cleaning the house, and I burst with happiness. And in their minds, they were in this terrible domestic rut.
Josh Lucas

I understood once I held a baby in my arms, why some people have the need to keep having them.
Spalding Gray

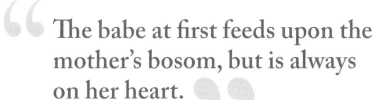

The babe at first feeds upon the mother's bosom, but is always on her heart.
Henry Ward Beecher

I think at a child's birth, if a mother could ask a fairy godmother to endow it with the most useful gift, that gift would be curiosity.

Eleanor Roosevelt

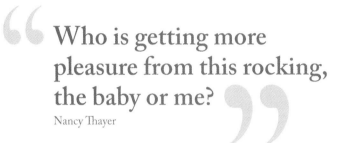

Who is getting more pleasure from this rocking, the baby or me?

Nancy Thayer

In the sheltered simplicity of the first days after a baby is born, one sees again the magical closed circle, the miraculous sense of two people existing only for each other.

Anne Morrow Lindbergh

I feel whole at last.

Meg Matthews

Our planning may leave something to be desired, but our designs, thank God, have been flawless.

Noor, Queen of Jordan, having given birth to her fourth child in six years

" There is nothing like a newborn baby to renew your spirit – and to buttress your resolve to make the world a better place. "

Virginia Kelley

Most of us would do more for our babies than we have ever been willing to do for anyone, even ourselves.

Polly Berrien Berends

I could still remember how having a two-day-old baby makes you feel faintly sorry for everyone else, stuck in their wan unmiraculous lives.

Marni Jackson

She made me a security blanket when I was born. That faded green blanket lasted just long enough for me to realize that the security part came from her.

Alexander Crane

" There are lots of things that you can brush under the carpet about yourself until you're faced with somebody whose needs won't be put off. "

Angela Carter, on being a mother for the first time, at age 43

It's sad that children cannot know their parents when they were younger; when they were loving, courting, and being nice to one another. By the time children are old enough to observe, the romance has all too often faded or gone underground.

Virginia Satir

Motherhood is mind-blowing.

Britney Spears

What good mothers... instinctively feel like
doing for their babies is usually best after all.

Benjamin Spock

Children seldom misquote you. They more often repeat word for word what you shouldn't have said.

Mae Maloo

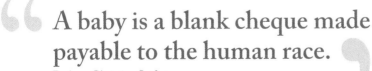

A baby is a blank cheque made payable to the human race.

Barbara Christine Seifert

Do not, on a rainy day, ask your child what he feels like doing, because I assure you that what he feels like doing, you won't feel like watching.

Fran Lebowitz

There is no reciprocity. Men love women, women love Children, children love hamsters.

Alice Thomas Ellis

 Don't tell your two-year-old she's driving you nuts. She just might say, 'Mama nuts' to everyone she meets.

Jan Blaustone

Children ask better questions than adults. 'May I have a cookie?' 'Why is the sky blue?' and 'What does a cow say?' are far more likely to elicit a cheerful response than 'Where is your manuscript?' 'Why haven't you called?' and 'Who's your lawyer?'

Fran Lebowitz

My kids always perceived the bathroom as a place where you wait it out until all the groceries are unloaded from the car.

Erma Bombeck

See the mind of a five-year-old as a volcano with two vents: destructiveness and creativeness.

Sylvia Aston Warner

Children are not things to be moulded, but are people to be unfolded.

Jess Lair

Children are like sponges; they absorb all your strength and leave you limp... But give them a squeeze and you get it all back.

Ann Van Tassells

Toddlers are more likely to eat healthy food if they find it on the floor.

Jan Blaustone

Perhaps parents would enjoy their children more if they stopped to realize that the film of childhood can never be run through for a second showing.

Evelyn Nown

Whether your child is 3 or 13, don't rush in to rescue him until you know he's done all he can to rescue himself.

Barbara F. Meltz

> Kids can be a pain in the neck when they're not a lump in your throat.
>
> Barbara Johnson

No animal is so inexhaustible as an excited infant.

Amy Leslie

People always talked about a mother's uncanny ability to read her children, but that was nothing compared to how children could read their mothers.

Anne Tyler

That's one thing I find about having children – it does unlock a door that separates you from other women who've had children.

Rebecca Miller

The illusions of childhood are necessary experiences; a child should not be denied a balloon because an adult knows that sooner or later it will burst.

Marcelene Cox

Likely as not, the child you can do least with will do the most to make you proud.

Mignon McLaughlin

I always wanted children, but not until they were actually part of my life did I realize that I could love that fiercely, or get that angry.

Cokie Roberts

To nourish children and raise them against odds is in any time, any place, more valuable than to fix bolts in cars or design nuclear weapons.

Marilyn French

" **What a difference it makes to come home to a child.** "

Mary McBride

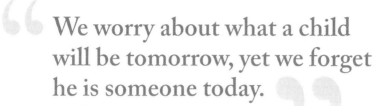

> We worry about what a child will be tomorrow, yet we forget he is someone today.
> Stacia Tauscher

The rules for parents are three... love, limit, and let them be.
Elaine M.Ward

My mother never gave up on me. I messed up in school so much they were sending me home, but my mother sent me right back.
Denzel Washington

> The mother's heart is the child's schoolroom.
> Henry Ward Beecher

A mother is neither cocky, nor proud, because she knows the school principal may call at any minute to report that her child had just driven a motorcycle through the gymnasium.
Mary Kay Blakely

Children learn to smile from their parents.

Shinichi Suzuki

You may have tangible wealth untold; caskets of jewels and coffers of gold. Richer than I you can never be, I had a mother who read to me.

Strickland Gillian

Never help a child with a task at which he feels he can succeed.

Maria Montessori

I never went to school beyond the third grade, but my mother taught me the difference between right and wrong.

Joe Lewis

Parents learn a lot from their children about coping with life.

Muriel Spark

I always tell people that I became a writer not because I went to school but because my mother took me to the library.

Sandra Cisneros

" Let France have good mothers, and she will have good sons. "

Napoleon Bonaparte

A man never sees all that his mother has been to him until it's too late to let her know that he sees it.

W.D. Howells

Snow and adolescence are the only problems that disappear if you ignore them long enough.

Earl Wilson

The God to whom little boys say their prayers has a
face very like their mothers.

James Matthew Barrie

My mother made me a scientist without ever intending to. Every other Jewish
mother in Brooklyn would ask her child after school: 'So? Did you learn
anything today?' But not my mother. 'Izzy,' she would say, 'did you ask a good
question today?'

Isidor Isaac Rabi

Who's a boy gonna talk to if
not his mother?

Donald E.Westlake

There was never a great man who had
not a great mother.

Olive Schreiner

" **Sooner or later
we all quote our
mothers.** "

Bern Williams

Men are what their mothers made them.

Ralph Waldo Emerson

Nobody can misunderstand a boy like his own mother.

Norman Douglas

My mother had a great deal of trouble with me, but I think she enjoyed it.

Mark Twain

My mother loved children – she would have given anything if I had been one.

Groucho Marx

When I was a child, my mother said to me, 'If you become a soldier, you'll be a general. If you become a monk you'll end up as the pope.' Instead I became a painter and wound up as Picasso.

Pablo Picasso

My idea of superwoman is someone who scrubs her own floors.

Bette Midler

When it comes to housework the one thing no book of household management can ever tell you is how to begin. Or maybe I mean why.

Katharine Whitehorn

I am thankful for a lawn that needs mowing, windows that need cleaning and gutters that need fixing because it means I have a home... I am thankful for the piles of laundry and ironing because it means my loved ones are nearby.

Nancie J. Carmody

Nature abhors a vacuum. And so do I.

Anne Gibbons

My second favourite household chore is ironing. My first being hitting my head on the top bunk until I faint.

Erma Bombeck

My mother is a walking miracle.

Leonardo DiCaprio

She is my first, great love. She was a wonderful, rare woman – you do not know; as strong, and steadfast, and generous as the sun. She could be as swift as a white whiplash, and as kind and gentle as warm rain, and as steadfast as the irreducible earth beneath us.

D. H. Lawrence

It seems to me that my mother was the most splendid woman I ever knew... I have met a lot of people knocking around the world since, but I have never met a more thoroughly refined woman than my mother. If I have amounted to anything, it will be due to her.

Charles Chaplin

Fifty-four years of love and tenderness and crossness and devotion and unswerving loyalty. Without her I could have achieved a quarter of what I have achieved, not only in terms of success and career, but in terms of personal happiness... She has never stood between me and my life, never tried to hold me too tightly, always let me go free...

Noël Coward

My mother has always been unhappy with what I do. She would rather I do something nicer, like be a bricklayer.

Mick Jagger

He wrote me sad Mother's Day stories. He'd always kill me in the stories and tell me how bad he felt about it. It was enough to bring a tear to a mother's eye.

Connie Zastoupil, mother of Quentin Tarantino

> The whole motivation for any performer is, 'Look at me, Ma!'
>
> Lenny Bruce

Looking back on my own childhood, after the infant years were over, I do not believe that I ever felt love for any mature person, except my mother...

George Orwell

As long as a woman can look ten years younger than her own daughter, she is perfectly satisfied.

Oscar Wilde

> Never grow a wishbone daughter, where your backbone ought to be.
>
> Clementine Paddleford

" A fluent tongue is the only thing a mother don't like her daughter to resemble her in. "

Richard Brinsley-Sheridan

My mother was very interested in giving her daughters the advantage of music and dance, if we had an interest in it. My father was not.

Suzanne Farrell

If my daughter Liza wants to become an actress, I'll do everything to help her.

Judy Garland

" To me, luxury is to be at home with my daughter, and the occasional massage doesn't hurt. "

Olivia Newton-John

There is a point when you aren't as much mom and daughter as you are adults and friends. It doesn't happen for everyone – but it did for mom and me.

Jamie Lee Curtis

What do girls do who haven't any mothers
to help them through their troubles?

Louisa May Alcott

A daughter reminds you of all the things you had forgotten about being young. Good and bad.

Maeve O'Reilly

The daughter never ever gives up on the mother, just as the mother never gives up on the daughter. There is a tie there so strong that nothing can break it.

Rachel Billington

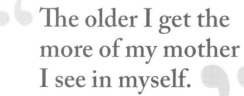

The older I get the more of my mother I see in myself.

Nancy Friday

> **Doesn't that show what an old man I am, when I can say to a mother 'I love your daughter,' and not get the reply 'What are your intentions, and what is your income?'**
>
> Lewis Carroll

My mother learned that she was carrying me at about the same time the Second World War was declared; with the family talent for magic realism, she once told me she had been to the doctor's on the very day.

Angela Carter

Unlike the mother–son relationship, a daughter's relationship with her mother is something akin to bungee diving... there is an invisible emotional cord that snaps her back.

Victoria Secunda

None but mothers know each other's feelings when we give up our daughters whom we love and cherish so tenderly to the mercies of a man, and perhaps even a stranger.

Emmeline B. Wells

There is only one certainty in the mother–daughter relationship: no matter how hard you try, mother will make mistakes and daughter will too, but the mistakes daughter makes will probably be all 'mother's fault'.

Faith Ringgold

Oh my son's my son till he gets him a wife, But my daughter's my daughter all her life.
Dinah Maria Mulock Craik

Being a child at home alone in the summer is a high-risk occupation. If you call your mother at work thirteen times an hour, she can hurt you.
Erma Bombeck

(My daughter) says she wants to marry a rich man, so she can have a Porsche. My rejoinder always is :'Go out and get rich yourself, so you can buy your own.'
Carol Royce

 My daughter thinks I'm nosy. At least that's what she says in her diary.
Sally Poplin

Of all the haunting moments of motherhood, few rank with hearing your own words come out of your daughter's mouth.
Victoria Secunda

The men who still have the largest share of the power in society don't do any domestic work. The very people who are making our most important decisions should know how to cook, know how to grow a garden, diaper a baby, and raise young people. They should not only know these things but practise them.
Susan Griffin

"Being a full-time mother is one of the highest salaried jobs... since the payment is pure love."
Mildred B. Vermont

The world is full of women blindsided by the unceasing demands of motherhood, still flabbergasted by how a job can be terrific and tortuous.
Anna Quindlen

"Working mother' is a misnomer... It implies that any mother without a definite career is lolling around eating bon-bons, reading novels, and watching soap opera."
Liz Smith

I can remember no time when I did not understand that my mother must write books because people would have and read them; but I cannot remember one hour in which her children needed her and did not find her.

Elizabeth Stuart Phelps

Motherhood is the biggest on-the-job training scheme in the world.

Erma Bombeck

If you would shut your door against the children for an hour a day and say: 'Mother is working on her five-act tragedy in blank verse!' you would be surprised how they would respect you. They would probably all become playwrights.

Brenda Ueland

... a business career for a woman and her need for a woman's life as wife and mother, are not enemies at all, unless we make them so.

Hortense Odlum

Nagging guilt is like grey paint splashed over
life's sparkling moments.

Sally Shannon

Career mothers are not kidding anybody.
Being a mom is the hardest job of all.

Sandy Duncan

When you combine wife, mother,
career and all, each role becomes the
perfect excuse for avoiding the worst
aspects of the other.

Bettina Arndt

I have spent so long erecting partitions around the part of me that writes –
learning how to close the door on it when ordinary life intervenes, how to
close the door on ordinary life when it's time to start writing again – that I'm
not sure I could fit the two parts of me back together now.

Anne Tyler

One of my children wrote in a third grade piece on how
her mother spent her time, 'one-half time on home, one-
half time on outside things, one-half time writing'.

Charlotte Montgomery

> **My job is quite suitable for full-time mothering.**
> Mare Winningham

Take motherhood: nobody ever thought of putting it on a moral pedestal until some brash feminists pointed out, about a century ago, that the pay is lousy and the career ladder non-existent.
Barabara Ehrenreich

Adults are always asking kids what they want to be when they grow up because they are looking for ideas.
Paula Poundstone

> **I want my children to have all the things I couldn't afford. Then I want to move in with them.**
> Phyllis Diller

Only mothers can think of the future, because they give birth to it in their children.
Maxim Gorky

> **Mama exhorted her children at every opportunity to 'Jump at de sun'. We might not land on the sun, but at least we would get off the ground.**
> Zora Neale Hurston

The mother loves her child most divinely, not when she surrounds him with comfort and anticipates his wants, but when she resolutely holds him to the highest standards and is content with nothing less than his best.
Hamilton Wright Mabie

If I have children I am going to make sure people don't ask them, 'Are you going to be an actor?' My mother said I could be anything I wanted except a policeman.
Kate Beckinsale

My mother wanted me to be her wings, to fly as she never quite had the courage to do. I love her for that. I love the fact that she wanted to give birth to her own wings.
Erica Jong

I would be most content if my children grew up to be the kind of people who think decorating consists mostly of building enough bookshelves.
Anna Quindlen

My mother married a very good man... and she
is not at all keen on my doing the same.

George Bernard Shaw

Youth fades; love droops; the leaves of friendship fall; a
mother's secret hope outlives them all.

Oliver Wendell Holmes Jr

You hear a lot of dialogue on the death of the American family.
Families aren't dying. They're merging into big conglomerates.

Erma Bombeck

Single women have a
dreadful propensity for
being poor. Which is one
very strong argument in
favour of matrimony.

Jane Austen

What is free time? I'm a single mother.
My free moments are filled with loving
my little girl.

Roma Downey

People talk about dysfunctional families; I've never seen any other kind.
Sue Grafton

Your basic extended family today includes your ex-husband or -wife, your ex's new mate, your new mate, possibly your new mate's ex and any new mate that your new mate's ex has acquired.
Delia Ephron

Yes, single-parent families are different from two-parent families. And urban families are different from rural ones, and families with six kids and a dog are different from one-child, no-pet households. But even if there is only one adult presiding at the dinner table, yours is every bit as much a real family as the Waltons.
Marge Kennedy

It's important for all single parents to remember that not everything that goes wrong, from your son's bad attitude towards school to the six holes in your teenage daughter's ear, is because you live in a single-parent home. Every family has its problems.
Marge Kennedy

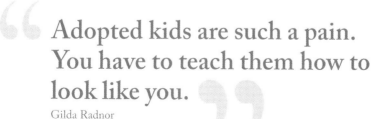

Adopted kids are such a pain. You have to teach them how to look like you.
Gilda Radnor

It helps when I can send my daughters off to their father's so I can support my new book with a national publicity tour. I started writing the book when my daughter was five. It took me almost four years.

Meg Tilly

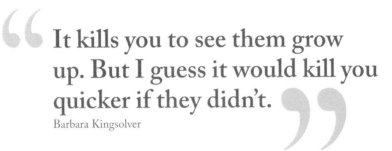

It kills you to see them grow up. But I guess it would kill you quicker if they didn't.

Barbara Kingsolver

The best way to keep children at home is to make the home atmosphere pleasant, and let the air out of the tyres.

Dorothy Parker

No matter how old a mother is, she watches her middle-aged children for signs of improvement.

Florida Scott-Maxwell

The successful mother sets her children free and becomes more free herself in the process.

Robert Havighurst

I take a very practical view of raising children, I put a sign in each of their rooms: checkout time is eighteen years.

Erma Bombeck

Most children threaten to run away from home. This is the only thing that keeps some parents going.

Phyllis Diller

You see much more of your children once they leave home.

Lucille Ball

If your children spend most of their time in other people's houses, you're lucky; if they all congregate at your house, you're blessed.

Mignon McLaughlin

" Until I got married, when I used to go out, my mother said goodbye to me as though I was emigrating. "

Thora Hird

When mothers talk about the depression of the empty nest, they're not mourning the passing of all those wet towels on the floor, or the music that numbs your teeth, or even the bottle of capless shampoo dribbling down the shower drain. They're upset because they've gone from supervisor of a child's life to a spectator. It's like being the vice president of the United States.

Erma Bombeck

Mothers need transfusions fairly often – phone calls, letters, bright postcards from the Outer Hebrides.

Heulwen Roberts

Kids are cute, babies are cute, puppies are cute. The little things are cute. See, nature did this on purpose so that we would want to take care of our young. Made them cute, tricked us. Then gradually they get older and older, until one day your mother sits you down and says, 'You know, I think you're ugly enough to get your own apartment.'

Cathy Ladman

Mothers are inclined to feel limp at 50. This is because the children have taken most of her stuffing to build their nests.

Samantha Armstrong

We are always the same age inside.

Gertrude Stein

If your baby is beautiful and perfect, never cries or fusses, sleeps on schedule and burps on demand, an angel all the time, you're the grandma.

Theresa Bloomingdale

Just about the time she thinks her work is done, she becomes a grandmother.

Edward H. Dreschnack

When a child is born, so are grandmothers.

Judith Levy

My grandmother was a very tough woman. She buried three husbands and two of them were just napping.

Rita Rudner

My grandmother is over 80 and still doesn't need glasses. Drinks right out of the bottle.

Henry Youngman

The simplest toy, one which even the youngest child can operate, is called a grandparent.

Sam Levenson

The best place to be when you're sad is your grandma's lap.

Jeannie, aged 7

If you want something expensive ask your grandma.

Matthew, aged 12

A grandmother pretends she doesn't know who you are on Halloween

Erma Bombeck

Becoming a grandmother is wonderful.
One moment you're just a mother. The
next you are all wise and prehistoric.

Pam Brown

It is as grandmothers that our mothers come into the fulness of their grace.
Christopher Morley

If becoming a grandmother was only a matter of choice, I should advise every one of you straight away to become one. There is no fun for old people like it.
Hannah Whithall Smith

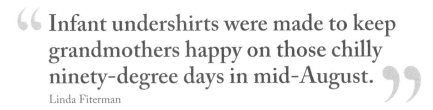

" Infant undershirts were made to keep grandmothers happy on those chilly ninety-degree days in mid-August. "
Linda Fiterman

You have to stay in shape. My grandmother, she started walking five miles a day when she was 60. She's 97 today and we don't know where the hell she is.
Ellen DeGeneres

My grandmothers are full of memories. Smelling of soap and onions and wet clay. With veins rolling roughly over quick hands. They have many clean words to say.
Margaret Walker

A mother becomes a true grandmother the day she stops noticing the terrible things her children do because she is so enchanted with the wonderful things her grandchildren do.

Lois Wyse

Soon I will be an old, white-haired lady, into whose lap someone places a baby, saying 'Smile, Grandma!' I, who myself was so recently photographed on my grandmother's lap.

Liv Ullmann

Your sons weren't made to like you. That's what grandchildren were for!

Jane Smiley

The proliferation of support groups suggests to me that too many Americans are growing up in homes that do not contain a grandmother. A home without a grandmother is like an egg without salt and Helpists know it.

Florence King

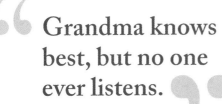

Grandma knows best, but no one ever listens.

Mary McBride

My mother's menu consisted of two choices: take it or leave it.

Buddy Hackett

When my mother had to get dinner for eight she'd just make enough for sixteen and only serve half.

Gracie Allen

My mother was a good recreational cook, but what she basically believed about cooking was that if you worked hard and prospered, someone else would do it for you.

Nora Ephron

Ask your child what he wants for dinner only if he is buying.

Fran Lebowitz

The most remarkable thing about my mother is that for thirty years she served the family nothing but leftovers. The original meal has never been found.

Calvin Trillin

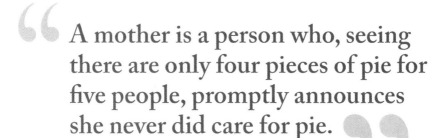

A mother is a person who, seeing there are only four pieces of pie for five people, promptly announces she never did care for pie.
Tenneva Jordan

As a mother I am often confused... One day I tell them to eat what they like, their bodies know intuitively what they need; and the next I say, 'OK, that's it – no more junk food in this house!'
Martha Boesing

My family can always tell when I'm well into a novel because the meals get very crummy.
Anne Tyler

Most turkeys taste better the day after; my mother's tasted better the day before.
Rita Rudner

I come from a family where gravy is considered a beverage.
Erma Bombeck

Early on, we equate being a good parent with how we feed our children. You're a 'good mother' if you feed your kid food that is healthy.
Goldie Alfasi

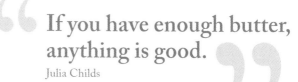

If you have enough butter, anything is good.
Julia Childs

And, indeed, is there not something holy about a great kitchen? ... the range like an altar... before which my mother bowed in perpetual homage, a fringe of sweat upon her upper lip and the fire glowing in her cheeks.
Angela Carter

My kids keep trying to convince me that there are two separate parts of their stomachs, one dedicated to dinner and the other to dessert.
Anna Quindlen

Motherhood is perhaps the only unpaid position
where failure to show up can result in arrest.

Mary Kay Blakely

Know that every mother occasionally feels 'at the end of her rope'. When you
reach the end of your rope, don't add guilt to your frustration. No one said
motherhood was going to be easy.'

Heather King

In childhood memories of every good cook, there's a large
kitchen, a warm stove, a simmering pot and a mom.

Barbara Costikyan

All of us have moments in our lives
that test our courage. Taking children
into a house with a white carpet is
one of them.

Erma Bombeck

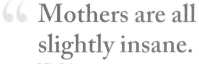 **Mothers are all
slightly insane.**

J.D. Salinger

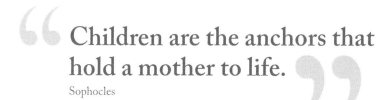

Children are the anchors that hold a mother to life.

Sophocles

I believe that always, or almost always, in all childhoods and in all the lives that follow them, the mother represents madness. Our mothers always remain the strangest, craziest people we've ever met.

Marguerite Duras

I used to be excellent. Since having a baby I couldn't tell you what day it is.

Gwyneth Paltrow

I tried to commit suicide by sticking my head in the oven, but there was a cake in it.

Lesley Boone

Housework is something that you do that nobody notices unless you haven't done it.

Sam Ewing

"**In raising my kids, I have lost my mind but found my soul.** "

Lisa T. Shepherd

Cleaning your house while the kids are still growing is like shovelling the walk before it stops snowing.

Phyllis Diller

My theory on housework is, if the item doesn't multiply, smell, catch fire, or block the refrigerator door, let it be. No one else cares. Why should you?

Erma Bombeck

"**My mother was an authority on pigsties. 'This is the worst-looking pigsty I have ever seen in my life and I want it cleaned up right now!'** "

Bill Cosby

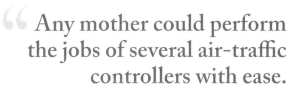 **Any mother could perform the jobs of several air-traffic controllers with ease.**

Lisa Alther

There's something wrong with a mother who washes out a measuring cup with soap and water after she's only measured water in it.

Erma Bombeck

Housework is a treadmill from futility to oblivion with stop-offs at tedium and counter-productivity.

Erma Bombeck

I hate housework! You make the beds, you do the dishes – and six months later you have to start all over again.

Joan Rivers

Neurotics build castles in the air, psychotics live in them. My mother cleans them.

Rita Rudner

No one ever died from sleeping in an unmade bed. I have known mothers who remake the bed after their children do it because there is a wrinkle in the spread or the blanket is on crooked. This is sick.
Erma Bombeck

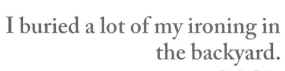

I buried a lot of my ironing in the backyard.
Phyllis Diller

Housekeeping is like being caught in a revolving door.
Marcelene Cox

I'm eighteen years behind in my ironing. There's no use doing it now, it doesn't fit anybody I know.
Phyllis Diller

The important thing about women today is, as they get older, they still keep house. It's one reason why they don't die, but men die when they retire. Women just polish the teacups.
Margaret Mead

At worst, a house unkempt cannot be so distressing as a life unlived.
Rose Macauley

" People can say what
they like about the
eternal verities, love
and truth and so
on, but nothing's as
eternal as the dishes. "

Margaret Mahy

Few tasks are more like the torture of Sisyphus than housework,
with its endless repetition: the clean becomes the soiled, the
soiled is made clean, over and over, day after day.

Simone De Beauvoir

If your house is really a mess and a stranger comes to the door greet
him with, 'Who could have done this? We have no enemies.'

Phyllis Diller

The worst thing about work in the house or home
is that whatever you do is destroyed, laid waste or
eaten within twenty-four hours.

Lady Hasluck

Have you ever taken anything out of the clothes basket because
it had become, relatively, the cleaner thing?
Katharine Whitehorn

Misery is when you make your bed and
then your mother tells you it's the day she's
changing the sheets.
Suzanne Heller

Now as always, the most automated appliance in a household is
the mother..
Beverley Jones

Motherhood is the great divide between one's own childhood
and adulthood. All at once someone is totally dependent upon
you. You are no longer the child of your mother but the mother
of your child.
Elaine Heffner

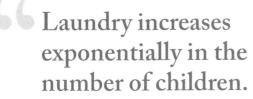

Laundry increases
exponentially in the
number of children.
Miriam Roberts

> # A sparkling house is a fine thing if the children aren't robbed of their lustre in keeping it that way.
> Marcelene Cox

Everybody wants to save the earth; nobody wants to help mom do the dishes.
P. J. O'Rourke

No one knows what her life expectancy is, but I have a horror of leaving this world and not having anyone in the entire family know how to replace a toilet tissue spindle.
Erma Bombeck

Behind every successful woman is a basket of dirty laundry.
Sally Forth

I may be the only mother in America who knows exactly what their child is up to all the time.
Barbara Bush

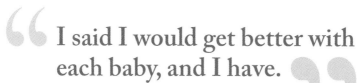

> **I said I would get better with each baby, and I have.**
> Demi Moore

When you are a mother, you are never really alone in your thoughts. A mother always has to think twice, once for herself and once for her child.
Sophia Loren

Motherhood has a very humanizing effect.
Everything gets reduced to essentials.
Meryl Streep

> **If you bungle raising your children, I don't think whatever else you do well matters very much.**
> Jacqueline Kennedy Onassis

Since I had the baby I can't tolerate anything violent or sad, I saw The Matrix and I had my eyes closed through a lot of it, though I didn't need to. I would peek, and then think, 'Oh OK, I can see that.'
Lisa Kudrow

I love being with my children. They're fascinating people.
Amy Grant

I love acting but it's much more fun taking the kids to the zoo.
Nicole Kidman

I've told Billy if I ever caught him cheating, I wouldn't kill him because I love his children and they need a dad. But I would beat him up. I know where all of his sports injuries are.
Angelina Jolie

You have to love your children unselfishly. That is hard. But it is the only way.
Barbara Bush

As a mother, you feel much more vulnerable. And when you're vulnerable, you're a much better actress.
Kate Beckinsale

I love being a mother... I am more aware. I feel things on a deeper level. I have a kind of understanding about my body, about being a woman.

Shelley Long

Being a mother has made my life complete.

Darcy Bussell

 **Children reinvent your world for you.**

Susan Sarandon

Then someone placed her in my arms. She looked up at me. The crying stopped. Her eyes melted through me, forging a connection in me with their soft heat.

Shirley Maclaine

When a child enters the world through you it alters everything on a psychic, psychological and purely practical level.

Jane Fonda

Because I am a mother, I am capable of being shocked: as I never was when I was not one.

Margaret Atwood

Don't call me an icon. I'm just a mother trying to help.

Princess Diana

**First things first,
second things never.**

Shirley Conran

Before I had a child I thought I knew all the boundaries of myself, that I understood the limits of my heart. It's extraordinary to have all those limits thrown out, to realize your love is inexhaustible.

Uma Thurman

**The easiest way to convince my kids
that they don't really need something
is to get it for them.**

Joan Collins

> **Once you become a mother, your heart is no longer yours... My daughter is the greatest thing I'll ever do in my life.**
>
> Kim Basinger

I'm very happy at home. I love to just hang out with my daughter, I love to work in my garden. I'm not a gaping hole of need.

Uma Thurman

> I know I could really kill for my daughter... It's like, that's my lair and nobody messes with my lair.
>
> Whitney Houston

> **I hope to leave my children a sense of empathy and pity and a will to right social wrongs.**
>
> Anita Roddick

It was no great tragedy being Judy Garland's daughter. I had tremendously interesting childhood years – except they had little to do with being a child.

Liza Minnelli

> **Motherhood is a wonderful thing. What a pity to waste it on the children.**
Judith Pugh

Is my mother my friend? I would have to say, first of all she is my Mother, with a capital 'M'; she's something sacred to me. I love her dearly... yes, she is also a good friend, someone I can talk openly with if I want to.
Sophia Loren

My mother phones daily to ask, 'Did you just try to reach me?' When I reply, 'No', she adds, 'So, if you're not too busy, call me while I'm still alive,' and hangs up.
Erma Bombeck

She tried in every way to understand me, and she succeeded. It was this deep, loving understanding as long as she lived that more than anything else helped and sustained me on my way to success.
Mae West

After my mother I never needed anyone else.
Mae West

My mother used to say that there are no strangers, only friends you haven't met yet. She's now in a maximum security twilight home in Australia.

Dame Edna Everage

My mother taught me to walk proud and tall 'as if the world was mine'.

Sophia Loren

My mother and I could always look out the same window without ever seeing the same thing.

Gloria Swanson

" My playground was the theatre. I'd sit and watch my mother pretend for a living. As a young girl, that's pretty seductive. "

Gwyneth Paltrow

I'm still that little girl who lisped and sat in the back of the car and threw vegetables at the back of mum's head when we drove home from the market. That never goes.

Tracey Ullman

One thing they never tell you about childraising is that for the rest of your life, at the drop of a hat, you will be expected to know your child's name and how old he or she is.

Erma Bombeck

There is possibly no guilt in this world to compare with leaving a sick child with a babysitter. The sitter could be Mother Theresa and you'd still feel rotten.

Erma Bombeck

My mother never saw the irony in calling me a son-of-a-bitch.

Jack Nicholson

He's a good boy; everything he steals he brings right home to his mother.

Fred Allen

Children are the most desirable opponents at Scrabble as they are both easy to beat and fun to cheat.

Fran Lebowitz

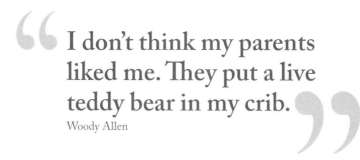

I don't think my parents liked me. They put a live teddy bear in my crib.

Woody Allen

The lullaby is the spell whereby the mother attempts to transform herself back from an ogre to a saint.

James Fenton

I've always been fascinated by the way that children and animals suffer stoically in a way that I don't think adults do.

Florida Scott-Maxwell

> When I was a little kid we had a sand box. It was a quicksand box. I was an only child... eventually.
>
> Stephen Wright

> My mother could make anybody feel guilty. She used to get letters of apology from people she didn't even know.
>
> Joan Rivers

She was a beautiful baby. She blew shining bubbles of sound. She loved motion, loved light, loved colour and music and textures. When she was just eight months old I had to leave her daytimes with the woman downstairs to whom she was no miracle at all.

Tille Olsen

We all have bad days... one mother admitted leaving the grocery store without her kids – 'I just forgot them. The manager found them in the frozen food isle, eating Eskimo pies.'

Mary Kay Blakely

> Sing out loud in the car even, or especially, if it embarrasses your children.
>
> Marilyn Penland

Mothers taken to the theatre when the kids are tiny phone the sitter in the interval to see if they are alive and happy. Mothers taken to the theatre when the kids are in their teens phone home to see if it's still standing.

Peter Gray

Women who cannot bear to be separated from their pet dogs send their children to boarding schools quite cheerfully.

George Bernard Shaw

I can't ever remember being affectionate with my mother in a spontaneous way... I always had a sort of horror of her. When I dreamed of my mother when I was a little boy, she was either selling me or coming at me with a knife. The latter came true later on.

Jurgen Bartsch

My mom said she learned how to swim. Her mother took her out in the lake and threw her off the boat. That's how she learned how to swim. I said, 'Mom, she wasn't trying to teach you how to swim.'

Paula Poundstone

My mother sent me to psychiatrists from the age of four because she didn't think little boys should be sad.

Andy Kaufman

One time I ran out of the store and took the bus home by myself after my mother asked a salesclerk where the 'underpants' counter was. Everyone in the store heard her. I had no choice.

Phyllis Theroux

I was always embarrassed because my mother wore flat pumps and a cosy jumper, while my friend's mums were punks or hippies.

Shirley Manson

" Seismic with laughter, gin and chicken helpless in her Irish hand. "

George Barker

My makeup wasn't smeared, I wasn't dishevelled, I behaved politely, and I never finished off a bottle, so how could I be alcoholic?

Betty Ford

" One reason I don't drink is that I want to know when I'm having a good time. "

Nancy Astor

Motherhood is the keystone of the arch of matrimonial happiness.

Thomas Jefferson

The story of a mother's life: Trapped between a scream and a hug.

Cathy Guisewite

My mother said I must always be intolerant of ignorance but understanding of illiteracy. That some people, unable to go to school, were more educated and more intelligent than college professors.

Maya Angelou

Children's talent to endure stems from their ignorance of alternatives.

Maya Angelou

If you want children to keep their feet on the ground, put some responsibility on their shoulders.

Abigail Van Buren

66 The biggest lesson we have to give our children is truth. 99

Goldie Hawn

My mother wanted me to understand that as a woman I could do pretty much whatever I wanted to, that I didn't have to use sex or sexuality to define myself.

Suzanne Vega

When your mother asks, 'Do you want a piece of advice?' it is a mere formality. It doesn't matter if you answer yes or no. You're going to get it anyway.

Erma Bombeck

Mom always tells me to celebrate everyone's uniqueness. I like the way that sounds.

Hilary Duff

At every step the child should be allowed to meet the real experience
of life; the thorns should never be plucked from his roses.
Ellen Key

From birth to 18 a girl needs good parents; from 18 to 35, she needs good
looks. From 35 to 55, good personality. From 55 on, she needs good cash. I'm
saving my money.
Sophie Tucker

My mother's best advice
to me was: 'Whatever you
decide to do in life, be sure
that the joy of doing it
does not depend upon the
applause of others, because
in the long run we are, all of
us, alone.'
Ali MacGraw

Mother always said that honesty
was the best policy, and money isn't
everything. She was wrong about
other things too.
Gerald Barzan

> ## Never have more children than you have car windows.
> Erma Bombeck

As a child you never quite understood how your mom was able to know exactly what you were thinking... Sometimes mom would know what you were thinking before the thought entered your head. 'Don't even think about punching your brother,' she would warn before you had time to make a fist.
Linda Sunshine

Giving advice comes naturally to mothers. Advice is in the genes along with blue eyes and red hair.
Lois Wyse

> ## Level with your child by being honest. Nobody spots a phoney quicker than a child.
> Mary MacCracken

When we as youngsters would accuse our mother of picking on us, her wise reply was, 'All you get from strangers is surface pleasantry or indifference. Only someone who loves you will criticize you.'
Judith Crist

> ## The best time to start giving your children money is when they will no longer eat it.
> Barbara Coloroso

For that's what a woman, a mother wants – to teach her children to take an interest in life. She knows it's safer for them to be interested in other people's happiness than to believe in their own.

Athenæus

... and moreover my mother told me as a boy (repeatedly) 'Ever to confess you're bored means you have no Inner Resources.' I conclude now I have no inner resources, because I am heavy bored.

John Berryman

Never play peek-a-boo with a child on a long plane trip. There's no end to the game. Finally I grabbed him by the bib and said, 'Look, it's always gonna be me!'

Rita Rudner

> ## Try to look at everything through the eyes of a child.
> Ruth Draper

Mother always told me, if you tell a lie, always rehearse it. If it don't sound good to you, it won't sound good to no one else.

Leroy 'Satchel' Paige

Listen carefully to what country people call mother wit. In those homely sayings are couched the collective wisdom of generations.

Maya Angelou

Everything I am or ever hope to be, I owe to my angel mother.

Abraham Lincoln

Yes, I care about my kids' problems, and I long to make suggestions. But these days I wait for children to ask for help, and I give it sparingly.

Susan Ferraro

My mama always used to tell me: if you can't find somethin' to live for, you best find somethin' to die for.

Tupac Shakur

A man loves his sweetheart the most, his wife the
best, but his mother the longest.

Irish proverb

A mother's love for her child is like nothing else in the world. It knows no law,
no pity, it dares all things and crushes down remorselessly all that stands in its
path.

Agatha Christie

When I stopped seeing my mother with the eyes of a child, I
saw the woman who helped me give birth to myself.

Nancy Friday

My mother was the most beautiful
woman I ever saw. All I am I owe to
my mother. I attribute all my success
in life to the moral, intellectual and
physical education I received from her.

George Washington

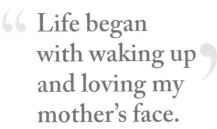

Life began
with waking up
and loving my
mother's face.

George Eliot

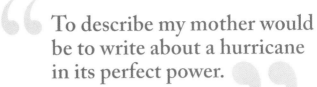

> To describe my mother would be to write about a hurricane in its perfect power.
>
> Maya Angelou

Mother love is the fuel that enables a normal human being to do the impossible.

Marion C. Garretty

> Mother – that was the bank where we deposited all our hurts and worries.
>
> T. DeWitt Talmage

Whatever else is unsure in this stinking dunghill of a world a mother's love is not.

James Joyce

> Who ran to help me when I fell, And would some pretty story tell, Or kiss the place to make it well? My mother.
>
> Ann Taylor

"Yes, mother. I can see you are flawed. You have not hidden it. That is your greatest gift to me."
Alice Walker

Nobody loves me but my mother, and she could be jivin' too.
B.B. King

In the beginning there was my mother. A shape. A shape and a force, standing in the light. You could see her energy; it was visible in the air. Against any background she stood out.
Marilyn Krysl

Motherhood is not for the faint-hearted. Frogs, skinned knees and the insults of teenage girls are not meant for the wimpy.
Danielle Steel

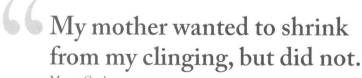

"My mother wanted to shrink from my clinging, but did not."
Mason Cooley

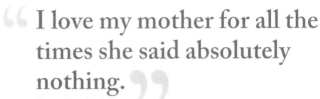 **I love my mother for all the times she said absolutely nothing.**

Erma Bombeck

I realized that, while I would never be my mother nor have her life, the lesson she had left me was that it was possible to love and care for a man and still have at your core a strength so great that you never even needed to put it on display.

Anna Quindlen

My mother read secondarily for information; she sank as a hedonist into novels. She read Dickens in the spirit in which she would have eloped with him.

Eudora Welty

Hugs can do great amounts of good – especially for children.

Princess Diana

Credits

The publishers would like to thank the following sources for their kind permission to reproduce the pictures in this book.

Getty Images: /Digital Vision: 10; /Dorling Kindersley: 3, 34; / Photodisc: 28; /Stockbyte: 22; /Taxi: 46

iStockphoto.com: 2, 4, 6, 9, 15, 18, 21, 24, 27, 31, 32, 45, 49, 52, 55, 58, 71, 72, 76, 79, 82, 85, 86, 89, 92, 95, 98, 101, 104, 111, 112, 119, 122, 125, 126

Thinkstock: /Brand X Pictures: 17, 63, 67, 120, 128; /Comstock: 11, 35, 80, 108; /Hemera: 12, 41, 61, 64, 74, 81, 91, 96, 103, 116, 121; / iStockphoto: 5, 16, 36, 39, 42, 50, 56, 57, 62, 68, 75, 90, 97, 102, 109, 114, 115; /Polka Dot: 107; /Stockbyte: 23, 29, 40, 51

Every effort has been made to acknowledge correctly and contact the source and or copyright holder of each picture and Carlton Books Limited apologises for any unintentional errors or omissions, which will be corrected in future editions of this book.